Incense and Insurrection

Glory!

Judson Cornwall

Psalm 42:1

Judson Cornwall, Th. D.

INCENSE AND INSURRECTION
© 1986 by Judson Cornwall, Th. D.
K Dimension Publishers
Atlanta, Georgia
All rights reserved.
Printed in the United States of America.
ISBN # 0-917-595-12-2

— 1 —

The Incense

The burning of incense as a means of worshipping God was not a part of the Hebrew heritage until after the exodus from Egypt. Actually, the use of incense in the worship of Jehovah was introduced by God Himself, on Mount Sinai, when He gave Moses the pattern for the Tabernacle with instructions for the ministry of the priesthood. Incense had long been used by other nations in their heathen worship, but Israel had not adopted their practice. In introducing the burning of incense as an act of worship, God made three specific differentiations from what Israel may have seen in idol worship. First, the incense was to be compounded from four principal spices; idol worship used only one fragrance at a time. Second, the incense was to be burned within the confines of the Tabernacle, and almost always on the Golden Altar in the Holy Place. Third, only the priesthood could offer this fragrant smoke of worship before the Lord. In later years Israel violated all of these restrictions by burning incense on their housetops to the Queen of Heaven, and God judged them sorely for it.

New Testament believers (with a few exceptions) no longer burn incense as an act of worship, any more than we observe the other rituals of the Tabernacle in the Wilderness; but we do, of course, enter into the spiritual reality of which the activities of the Tabernacle were a type or picture.

Incense speaks of the vocal end of our worship. John called it "the prayers of the saints" (*see* Revelation 5:8). Most Bible commentators speak of the incense as being intercessory prayer, and there may be times when this is so, but this greatly limits our concepts of approaching God, for heartfelt prayer is far more than just intercession. Actually, there are at least eight forms or levels of prayer pictured in the New Testament. In ascending order, they are:

1. The sinner's prayer ["Lord, be merciful to me a sinner"]
2. Petition ["Give us . . ."—the Lord's prayer]
3. Supplication [literally, "to bend or stoop in kindness before a superior"]
4. Intercession [coming between God's righteous wrath and sinning man]
5. Submission ["Make me"]
6. Thanksgiving [for what God has done—His performance]
7. Praise [for Who God is—His Person]
8. Worship and adoration [love poured out; relationship enjoyed]

Incense may refer to all these levels of prayer, but because the incense was burned on the Golden Altar right in front of the veil, I conceive it depicting the highest form of prayer, which is worship and adoration. The burning of incense was the one action of the priest that ministered unto God Himself; all other actions were on behalf of the people or the priests themselves.

For example, the Brazen Altar was for sin; it effected justification. The Laver was for the continual cleansing of the functioning priests, and speaks of the work of sanctification. The Lampstand, which was for illumination, revealed all the activities of the Holy Place, while the Table of Shewbread effected fellowship among the priestly brotherhood. All these pieces of furniture which formed stations of worship were for the sake of the priest and his ministrations, but the little Golden Altar of Incense, which sat right next to the veil in a position as close to the Ark of the Covenant as a priest could attain except on the Day of Atonement, was used for relating to God. The incense that was burned there daily went through the veil into God's presence and also filled the priestly compartment with its fragrant odor, making both God and man aware of an existing fellowship and communion between themselves.

The Altar of Incense was high-level communication and communion with God, so it certainly must rise higher than constant petitioning—whether for ourselves or for others—for the relationship between a suppliant and a supplier is hardly a love relationship. Since true worship is not getting from God but giving to God, the burning of incense was more an act of worship than an act of petitioning, for incense gives of itself when it is burned and gets nothing in return for its offering.

At Sinai, God provided that this incense would be burned continually in the Holy Place upon the Golden Altar, but on at least two occasions He instructed Aaron to bring some of the incense out among the congregation in the portable censer that was used on the Day of Atonement to take incense into the Holy of Holies. Both of these occasions are described in the sixteenth chapter of Numbers. This was the first opportunity for the Israelites to directly smell the sweet fragrance of the incense that was compounded to the Divine formula; before that time they had smelled only the residue of the incense that remained in the hair and on the garments of the officiating priests.

This should have been a grand occasion for celebration, for God's highest symbol of worship was coming out among His people. Unfortunately, however, it was not a festive event. The action of the people that provoked God to have Aaron bring the incense of worship from the Holy Place to the congregation was severe insurrection against Divinely-appointed leadership. There are times when the private act of worship is chosen by God to become a public demonstration of whose side we are on, for worship, far more than any other religious activity, reveals the inner attitudes of our lives and God's acceptance or rejection of our ways.

Now Korah the son of Izhar, the son of Kohath, the son of Levi, with Dathan and Abiram the sons of Eliab, and On the son of Peleth, sons of Reuben, took men; and they rose up before Moses with some of the children of Israel, two hundred and fifty leaders of the congregation, representatives of the congregation, men of renown. They gathered together against Moses and Aaron, and said to them, "You take too much upon yourselves, for all the congregation is holy, every one of them, and the LORD is among them. Why then do you exalt yourselves above the congregation of the LORD?"

So when Moses heard it, he fell on his face; and he spoke to Korah and all his company, saying, "Tomorrow morning the LORD will show who is His and who is holy, and will cause him to come near to Him; that one whom He chooses He will cause to come near to Him. Do this: Take censers, Korah and all your company; put fire in them and put incense in them before the LORD tomorrow, and it shall be that the man whom the LORD chooses shall be the holy one. You take too much upon yourselves, you sons of Levi!"

Then Moses said to Korah, "Hear now, you sons of Levi: Is it a small thing to you that the God of Israel has separated you from the congregation of Israel, to bring you near to Himself, to do the work of the tabernacle of the LORD, and to stand before the congregation to serve them; and that He has brought you near to Himself, you and all your brethren, the sons of Levi, with you? And are you seeking the priesthood also? Therefore you and all your company are gathered together against the LORD. And what is Aaron that you murmur against him?"

And Moses sent to call Dathan and Abiram the sons of Eliab, but they said, "We will not come up! Is it a small thing that you have brought us up out of a land flowing with milk and honey, to kill us in the wilderness, that you should keep acting like a prince over us? Moreover you have not brought us into a land flowing with milk and honey, nor given us inheritance of fields and vineyards. Will you put out the eyes of these men? We will not come up!"

Then Moses was very angry, and said to the LORD, "Do not respect their offering. I have not taken one donkey from them, nor have I hurt one of them."

—(Numbers 16:1-15)

— 2 —

The Insurrection

In a democracy, the ballot box allows the ambitious office-seeker to challenge the incumbent, but in a theocracy, where all positions are filled by Divine appointment, some sort of over-throw seems necessary for one to gain another's office. Jude 11 holds Korah responsible for Israel's most severe insurrection, while Numbers 16 lists three co-conspirators: Korah, Dathan, and Abiram. It seems that Korah challenged Moses' and Aaron's ecclesiastical leadership, while Dathan and Abiram challenged Moses' civil authority. Dathan and Abiram seemed so unconcerned over the ecclesiastical leadership that they refused to even come to the Tabernacle to talk with Moses there.

This proved to be the most serious mutiny Moses had to face during the forty years in the wilderness. Other insurrections involved only a few persons, were not organized, and lacked key leadership, but this one had all three of these elements. Korah demonstrated great leadership ability and a keen mind in staging this rebellion. He had it well thought out, well planned, and well organized, and so he was able to simply stand back and let others do the "dirty work" in the rebellion while he "waited in the wings" to take over the ecclesiastical leadership of the nation.

Korah belonged to the same Kohathite sub-tribe as Moses and Aaron, and they were related by some sort of cousinship, for Korah's father, Izhan, was the elder brother of Amram, Moses' father. Perhaps there was a sense of commonality and equality by relationship that made it difficult for Korah to respect Moses' position in leadership. "Familiarity breeds contempt" is more than an epigram; it often becomes a reality. Just as the citizens of Christ's home town had difficulty accepting His Messiahship, so friends and relatives of pastors today often have difficulty accepting God's appointment of a member of their family as the spiritual head and authority in the Body of Christ.

As is common with all leaders of rebellion, Korah realized that his single voice would be insufficient to effect change, so he began to systematically mobilize others into his conspiracy. I read that in addition to Dathan and Abiram, Korah succeeded in gathering 250 leaders of the congregation into his cause. They are called "representatives of the congregation, men of renown" (Numbers 16:1). Furthermore, a little later "Korah gathered all the congregation against them [Moses and Aaron] at the door of the tabernacle of meeting" (Numbers 16:19). Like leaven in bread dough, one man's dissatisfaction fermented mutiny throughout the entire camp. Perhaps few things are more contagious than rebellion, for, short of the work of grace in our lives, all of us are inherently rebels. We want our own way at any cost. Isaiah 53:6 firmly attests this: "All we like sheep have gone astray; we have turned, every one, to his own way . . . ."

Perhaps we could give Korah the benefit of the doubt and say that originally he may well have been sincere. Somehow he had convinced himself that Moses and Aaron were usurpers. It is possible that he began his agitation without any thought of advantage for himself, but when he gained a following with popular applause, the pride of leadership and the excitement of conflict drove him to the extremity of self-exaltation, so that it was no longer "Moses is wrong" but "I am right!"

Korah and his followers sought the priesthood because they affirmed it to be the common possession of all Israelites. Not content to serve on the team as a Levite associate of Aaron, Korah wanted to be promoted to Aaron's level in ministry. What a valuable helper in the Kingdom of God Korah might have been! He could easily have become a "second" to Joshua, and perhaps could have stepped into Joshua's place when Joshua replaced Moses. Instead of that, Korah led the wretched life of a conspirator, and came to a bad end which left behind him an infamous name.

A few years ago my wife and I were ministering in a church that was pastored by a promising young man whom we had known when he was an associate pastor. Everything this young man knew, he had learned by on-the-job training under an older man. While we were there, this older pastor contacted the young pastor, saying that retirement age was upon him and he was looking for someone to take his place in leadership of the local congregation. He asked this young man to return and serve with him as an associate while the older man gently gave him more and more responsibility and authority until the older pastor could completely step out of the church and give his final years to a traveling ministry.

The young man counseled with me about this, and I encouraged him to take the offer, for I felt that he could not in many years develop on his own what was virtually being handed to him on a silver platter. I could foresee no great problems, for both men embraced similar religious philosophies and expressions.

Tragically, however, within a few weeks of his installation as the associate to the pastor, the discontented members of the congregation (and there are some in every congregation) succeeded in getting both his attention and his heart, and he led a revolt against the very man he had come to replace. Unwilling to wait for the season of transfer of power, he opted to establish himself as "king" through congregational revolution. He failed, and although dealt with most graciously by the pastor, he is now out of the ministry, and the local congregation suffered greatly for several years.

Here was a modern Korah who was so discontented with the high calling of God for his life that he rebelled against the person who had a higher calling, in hopes of attaining that position forcefully. In his failure he lost the place that God had given him. The sorrow of this story is that it is merely representative of hundreds of such incidents that occur annually in American churches.

Discontent with our place in the Body of Christ pollutes our worship. The desire to be seen, to be honored, to be promoted, is rooted in pride, which always prevents true worship. God wants to be worshipped in humility and submission, not in self-exaltation and self-promotion. Covetousness, whether of things, position or power, is a disqualifying sin which successfully prevents true worship of God. As Dr. Scofield used to say, "Discontent with the provisions and promises of God is the blighted fruit of a doubting soul."

Korah's desire became a deed which ended in an act of civil rebellion. He challenged Moses and Aaron, " 'You take too much upon yourselves' " (verse 3). The *Targum Palestine* interprets this as "You have enjoyed power long enough." There can be no question that Korah's purpose was to replace Aaron with himself. All his cries of "equality" are now seen to be sham. He didn't want equality; he wanted superiority—his superiority. Korah wanted a position far above that of equality with the people of Israel; he wanted the same power of the man he was trying to dispossess with the battle cry of "equality."

This must have been doubly painful for Aaron, for several months prior to this he had joined Miriam, his sister, in the same cry against Moses. Isn't it interesting how the chickens come home to roost, and what you have done is done unto you? Aaron, who had told Moses, "You think you're the only prophet around here? I, too, prophesy," now faced Korah, who declared absolute equality of priesthood—"I'm as big as you are."

Over the years I have consistently warned men who were rising up in rebellion against leadership that even if they succeeded, others would rise up against them, for it is a law in the Kingdom that what you sow, you reap. When Judah fought against the Canaanites, they captured their king, Adoni-Bezek, "and cut off his thumbs and big toes. And Adoni-Bezek said, 'Seventy kings with their thumbs and big toes cut off used to gather their food under my table; as I have done, so God has repaid me' " (Judges 1:6,7). It seems irrevocable that if you start chopping off thumbs, you, in turn, will lose your thumbs also.

Rebellion is an outer manifestation of an inner attitude. What was a thought becomes an action. How wisely does the

New Testament warn us to guard our minds; Jesus Himself said, " 'Out of the abundance of the heart the mouth speaks' " (Matthew 12:34). Every deed started as a desire which began as a concept. Korah mulled this over in his mind, then talked it over in his fellowship, and before long what had been a concept was now in control of him, forcing him into rebellion against God's leadership.

If Korah had rebelled on his own, or had it been just Korah, Dathan, and Abiram, perhaps neither the insurrection nor God's punishment would have been so severe, for when previously it had been just Miriam and Aaron contesting Moses face to face, it never created an issue in the camp, and God merely smote Miriam with leprosy for a short season. But Korah's rebellion deliberately involved others—many others. This chapter begins, "Now Korah . . . took men; and he rose up before Moses" (verse 1). The second verse tells us that these men that he took with him in his rebellion were the 250 **leaders** of the congregation, **representatives** of the congregation, and **men of renown**. Korah ensnared the eldership, the presbytery, and the board of deacons of that congregation with his cry of "equality." He so successfully poisoned the minds of these leaders that, as with Absalom of old, they felt that they would rather follow a different leader they did not know than remain with the leader they did know. It is tragic, but consistent with humans, that most of us would rather follow a leader we do not know. Somehow we mislabel "hope" as "faith" in the unknown, whereas faith, being rooted in fact, demands something that is known.

Korah was able not only to stir the leadership into revolt but, through that leadership, was able to rouse the people to mutiny, for with the congregation's key leadership in revolt, it is almost to be expected that the congregation would join them against

Moses. Korah, who had never brought Israel deliverance, had never produced manna, had never opened a rock to bring forth water, and had never been in the presence of God to hear the voice of God or to see the face of God, as had Moses, could stir the entire community against the man who had wrought these great miracles. And he did it merely by promising them greater power, rank, and prominence. One of the heartbreaks of leaders is the short memories of those who have benefited by that leadership. In less than a year, these former slaves wanted to replace their emancipator with themselves.

Unfortunately, this did not cease when Israel entered the promised land. Human nature, even after regeneration, remains quite unchanged even to this day.

Quite recently I shared lunch with a pastor who told me of a young man who had been saved through his ministry. The pastor had taken this young man into his heart and had discipled and trained him for several years. His rapid maturity and developing leadership abilities caught the attention of the congregation, and they eventually elected him to serve as a deacon. The very week after the business meeting, the young man came into the pastor's study to ask, "Pastor, now that I have been elected to the deacon board, what is my authority over you?" How quickly the disciple became the discipler in his own eyes. The son in the faith felt that he must exercise authority over his father in the faith.

It is little wonder that many pastors are terrified of giving leadership opportunities to members of the congregation. Like Korah, many cannot conceive of themselves as members of the team. Even a minor position or title in the church seems to engender a lust for major authority. And, like Korah, this is often expressed with the cry of "equality."

Discontent with our position in life may get us into trouble, but rebellion against God's appointed leadership always drags those closest to us into our dissension. How many children have turned from God and the church because of the rebellion of their parents over some issue that arose in the church? Eternity alone will reveal the number of new converts who have died of neglect because a zealous rebel got hold of them before they had a chance to become grounded in the ways of God. We not only do not live or die unto ourselves; we cannot rebel unto ourselves, for a successful rebellion must become powerful, and that requires people, so we consistently drag others into our rebellion.

All over America I continue to see church "splits" that are the result of rebellion! The issue is usually minor. Actually, it is rare to find a church issue sufficiently large to justify division. But though the issue is small, the rebellion becomes severe, and the casualties are many and often eternal.

Perhaps Americans need to be reminded of God's severe attitude toward rebellion. God told Hananiah the prophet, " 'This year you shall die, because you have taught rebellion against the LORD' " (Jeremiah 28:16), and in less than a year Hananiah was dead and buried. To Shemaiah, a false prophet, God said, " 'He shall not have anyone to dwell among this people, nor shall he see the good that I will do for My people , . . . because he has taught rebellion against the LORD' " (Jeremiah 29:32).

Frankly, rebellion is vented anger. It is frustration expressed, but it often goes beyond these bounds. Samuel told king Saul, " 'Rebellion is as the sin of witchcraft' " (1 Samuel 15:23). In the Old Testament, witchcraft was punishable by death. There was no parole. God showed no mercy for witchcraft, for it is an attempt to bring the supernatural into our affairs without having to submit to the Divine. Tragically, we again have a generation that is looking to witchcraft. They want the supernatural, but they do not want God. Similarly, in religious leadership there are those who want the top positions of authority without having the relationship with God, from Whom such appointments come.

Korah's rebellion seemed to be against Moses and Aaron, but it was in fact against God. Korah enlisted the aid of others to lower Moses in order to exalt himself, without realizing that God viewed this as a frontal attack against Himself. Beautifully, Moses, the meekest of all men, did not answer Korah's accusation; he went directly to God. Until God spoke to him, Moses said nothing. Korah had united the people with the rallying cry of "equality," and the truth of this cry made it almost impossible for Moses to answer, for had not God Himself, on Mount Sinai, said, " 'You shall be to Me a kingdom of priests and a holy nation' " (Exodus 19:6)? Korah grabbed this statement as his text and preached it throughout Israel's leadership, looking for all who were dissatisfied with anything. Regardless of the basis of their discontent, Korah said, in effect, "Our real problem is that we've missed God. God said that we are equal, and yet we're submitted to Moses and Aaron, and they are lording it over us."

The lust for power—the determination to be the greatest—has been the ruin of many a richly-gifted man. Such men fail to realize that in attacking God-appointed leadership, they unwittingly oppose God, and He is a formidable foe! "Climbing the ladder of success" almost always involves stepping on others on the way up, and often being stepped on by them on our way down.

But this is the world's way to "success." Divine promotion does not necessitate human demotion. In the world, to become a senator you must dispossess an officeholder, but in the Kingdom of God, to become a priest you need not replace a priest. Twice the book of Revelation declares that Christ Jesus "has made us kings and priests to His God and Father" (Revelation 1:6, 5:10), and on both occasions the offices are spoken of as plural—kings **and** priests. There is sufficient room in God's harvest field for all qualified workers. God, the Master Planner, chooses whom He wills, to be where He wills, doing what He wills, as long as He wills, and the first step to successful Christian service is to wholeheartedly accept that principle. The moment the choice becomes yours, both you and the Body of Christ are in for trouble.

God is more eager to promote us than we are to be promoted. However, God insists upon sufficient spiritual maturity in us to be able to function in the higher level of service without being destroyed in it before He'll ever promote us. Ambition, ability and willingness are not the important keys to promotion—holiness and maturity are. If we must tear down another in order to rise to our ministries, it is evidence that we lack spiritual holiness and maturity, and God dares not give promotion to us.

And Moses said to Korah, "Tomorrow, you and all your company be present before the LORD—you and they, as well as Aaron. Each of you take his censer and put incense in it, and each of you bring his censer before the LORD, two hundred and fifty censers; you also, and Aaron, each of you with his censer."

So every man took his censer, put fire in it, laid incense on it, and stood at the door of the tabernacle of meeting with Moses and Aaron. And Korah gathered all the congregation against them at the door of the tabernacle of meeting. Then the glory of the LORD appeared to all the congregation. And the LORD spoke to Moses and Aaron, saying, "Separate yourselves from among this congregation, that I may consume them in a moment."

Then they fell on their faces, and said, "O God, the God of the spirits of all flesh, shall one man sin, and You be angry with all the congregation?" So the LORD spoke to Moses, saying, "Speak to the congregation, saying, 'Get away from the tents of Korah, Dathan, and Abiram.'"

Then Moses rose and went to Dathan and Abiram, and the elders of Israel followed him. And he spoke to the congregation, saying, "Depart now from the tents of these wicked men! Touch nothing of theirs, lest you be consumed in all their sins."

—(Numbers 16:16-26)

— 3 —

The Indictment

Power politics in the local church are extremely stressful to pastors, and Moses was no exception. As he lay prostrate before the Lord (verse 4), Moses received Divine instructions for handling the crisis. " 'Do this' God said: ' "Take censers, Korah and all your company; put fire in them and put incense in them before the LORD tomorrow, and it shall be that the man whom the LORD chooses shall be the holy one' " (Numbers 16:6,7). Basically God said, "Okay, Korah. You want to be the high priest? Be My guest. Try it! Take incense and function like a high priest."

How much easier it is to sit in the stands yelling instructions to the team than it is to suit up and get in the middle of the football game. Many persons are professional Monday-morning critics of their pastor. Maybe they just need to walk in his shoes for a season. If they could listen to the garbage handed to their pastor in the counseling room all week long, they would be amazed that he could preach anything decent on Sunday morning. Few members of the congregation have even the faintest comprehension of the emotional load pastors carry in being responsible not only for the congregation but for the financial program, the building program, the staff, and all of the ministries of the church. Still, many who have no more responsibility in the church than to arrive on time on Sunday morning sit back as professional Korahs, musing, "Pastor, you take too much on yourself. I'm as good as you are."

Over and over again during the nearly thirty years that I pastored, persons from my congregations would approach me with criticisms of the church program, my methods of pastoring or our spiritual emphasis. I would respond by saying, "You're probably right. Why don't you go out and start your own church, and do it your way. Go try it!" My advice was not heeded, of course, for it is far easier to tear down what another has built than to build on your own.

We live in a destructive generation of persons who seem to delight in defacing and tearing down, and yet lack the capacity and the willingness to apply themselves to build or develop anything. This same spirit of the age comes into the Church. We often feel justified in being the official critic of everything that is being done, and in defaming, defacing, or destroying what another has done. In using ourselves as the standard of correctness, we tend to destroy everything that is unlike ourselves, totally forgetting that different is not necessarily inferior—it is just different.

One of the dangers of insisting upon your "rights" is that God may grant them to you, to your own destruction. Korah and these men wanted to function in the high priestly office, so God said, "Petition granted—according to your will, not My will."

We cannot help wondering how many men are in religious service under this same Divine permission.

It is fairly easy to prove our equality or even superiority before the people, but that does not constitute Divine choice. People may applaud your championing their cause, but nothing will disqualify a person from spiritual leadership more rapidly than pride, unless it would be lust. In Korah we see a pride-filled man, lusting for another's position, daring to come before the Lord saying, "I'm as great as Moses and Aaron." God's response was simply "Not in My sight, you're not!" Jesus declared that " 'whoever exalts himself will be abased, and he who humbles himself will be exalted' " (Matthew 23:12).

Korah, who was preaching "equality," readily accepted God's challenge to prove that he could offer incense as well as Aaron. What he and his co-conspirators didn't seem to realize was that God has made a differentiation between **position** and **performance** in His Church. Many can preach, but God chooses one to be the pastor. "You can all prophesy," Paul said (1 Corinthians 14:31), but that doesn't make all of us prophets. Operation of gifts does not produce office in the Church.

It has often seemed that some whom God chooses appear to be less qualified than some who are not chosen, but they are still God's choice. We are not working in a democracy in the Church of Jesus Christ. Office is not achieved through popularity or ability. Appointments are a Divine prerogative, for we serve in a theocracy. If God chooses a less capable person, then it becomes His responsibility to make that person able. It is never our responsibility to push him aside because someone who has a better education, more talents, or a more appealing personality seems to outshine the one whom God has chosen. Regardless of anyone's ability to "shine," that doesn't put that person into office.

God told Moses to tell Korah, " 'Tomorrow, you and all your company be present before the LORD—you and they, as well as Aaron' " (Numbers 16:16). Korah, who had never met God, wanted to minister unto God as the high priest, so God granted him an audience to find out what it is like to stand in the presence of a holy God. We may seem equal to leadership in front of the people, but the true test comes when we function before the Lord. Issues of rebellion are best settled in God's presence, not in the board room.

God was proposing a test whereby His choice would be made known to all Israel, and since Korah's issue was the ecclesiastical leadership, God chose the highest function of the priestly office for the test: the burning of incense. Worship became the point of decision! As a Levite, Korah could take care of all of the Outer Court ministries; it was just the ministry unto God in the Holy Place that was withheld from him. When this became the thing Korah lusted after, God said, "All right, let him do it." By Divine decree it was to be Korah and his 250 leaders versus Aaron. This was not too unlike the situation of Elijah on Mount Carmel when he stood alone versus the 450 prophets of Baal. In both cases the manpower was insignificant; it was God's answer that mattered.

Korah and his followers were granted Divine permission to function as Aaronic priests, but from the moment they got their own way, everything they did was wrong! To begin with, they had the wrong censers. God had prescribed that the censers to be used in the Holy Place and the Holy of Holies were to be made of pure gold, but Korah and company made theirs of brass (or, more probably, bronze). No doubt all the gold which they had brought out of Egypt had gone into the construction of the golden calf some months before. In the Old Testament, gold speaks of Divine glory manifested, while bronze speaks of

Divine judgment endured. The high priest was to demonstrate God's evident glory; yet here came these usurper priests manifesting God's judgment. I suppose that it is not possible to manifest something we have never seen. These Levites well knew the ministry of the Brazen [bronze] Altar, but they knew nothing of the ministry of the Golden Lampstand, the Table or the Altar in the Holy Place. I have observed that self-appointees tend to demonstrate bronze rather than gold; they often major in "hell-fire and brimstone" rather than in "mercy and truth."

Counterfeit instruments of worship become poor containers for offering true worship unto God. It is always easier to see what another does and copy it than it is to pay the price to get what that worshipper has received from God. Brass is a cheaper commodity than gold, and is usually molded into shape rather than beaten into form, as is gold. "Cheap worship" just doesn't make points with God. The sooner we learn this, the sooner we will learn true worship.

"But," you may argue, "God told them to take the censers." Yes, just as He has told us to take music as an implement through which we offer worship to Him, but unless that music is "pure gold," it will restrict rather than release our worship. All attempts to "Christianize" the world's music seem to end in bronze censers. From time to time we see popular entertainers of the world coming into a salvation experience and using their talents to entertain Christians in the churches instead of sinners in the stadiums. They wear the same clothing, play and sing the same type of music, and use the same gestures and trappings they did when they were in the world, but because the lyrics have been changed to include God's name, we are led to believe they are offering incense of worship to God in golden censers. Somehow it seems to me that they are putting on the same show they did for the world, for the same reasons: money and fame. Just because the lyrics are now "Christian" doesn't make the music golden.

Heaven is full of music, and Paul taught that the believer is full of music. In Ephesians he declared that the point of overflow for the Spirit in a believer is melody: "Be filled with the Spirit, speaking to one another in psalms and hymns and spiritual songs, singing and making melody in your hearts to the Lord" (Ephesians 5:18,19). Later he declared that being full of God's Word will be evidenced with the music of the Spirit: "Let the word of Christ dwell in you richly in all wisdom, teaching and admonishing one another in psalms and hymns and spiritual songs, singing with grace in your hearts to the Lord" (Colossians 3:16). We need not bring bronze to the Lord when gold is inherent within us. Even the world's best is inferior to heaven's worst. Bronze censers will never make our worship acceptable to God.

These ambitious rebels not only had the wrong kind of censers; they also had the wrong fire inside those censers. God had been very specific as to the source for the fire that would ignite the incense before His presence. He commanded that coals be taken from the Brazen Altar, for that fire had been started by God Himself on the day that the Tabernacle was put into Divine service. Only Korah, of all the insurgents, had access to the Brazen Altar, and in his current state of rebellion it is doubtful that he would take 251 coals of fire from the Altar. Like the sons of Aaron on the day the Tabernacle was dedicated, these usurper priests had to offer their incense with "strange fire," that is, fire from a source other than Divine. Divine fire comes only from God's presence, and only those who have found an entrance to God will ever have the fire of God in their lives.

Worship that is not ignited by the Divine presence is unacceptable to God. How easy it is for us to bring the stadium enthusiasm into the place of worship and substitute applause for praise, emotion for devotion, and action for adoration while declaring that we have worshipped God, but it will be unacceptable worship in God's eyes. Our pans were brass, and our flames were self-ignited. Nothing kindled in the human emotions can substitute for the fire of God in man's spirit! The incense of true worship must be ignited by God. How easily we can conform to another's performance without ever catching his fervor. We often get involved in another's warmth and smoke and think that we have his fire, but Divine fire comes only from the Divine.

I have repeatedly observed that a congregation who has a pastor who is genuinely ablaze with the fire of God tends to enter into the anointing and flame of their pastor. But if they move to another location, or the pastor is moved to another church, they quickly become little more than charred wood. They have not learned to receive the fire of God for themselves; they have merely drawn close to the one who had that fire. God alone is the source of Divine fire. It is not passed on from person to person; it is ignited by God's interaction with each person.

These proud mutineers not only found themselves stuck with the wrong censers and wrong fire, but it soon became evident that they also had the wrong incense. God had given a specific formula that blended four spices into a compound which became the Divine incense. Although they had spent months setting up this rebellion, God gave them only from one night until the next morning to prepare for this test to determine who would be the high priest. Even if they had known the formula for the incense (which they couldn't), there would not have been enough time to secure the spices, since none of the spices was native to the wilderness; so they had to get their incense

27

wherever they could. The heathen inhabitants of the nations all around Israel used incense in the worship of their gods, but they burned only one spice at a time. Possibly the Israelites brought some Egyptian incense with them on their exodus. Whatever the source was, these pretenders to the priesthood brought false incense to be offered on false fire in the wrong kind of censers.

The true incense of worship is a blend of consecration, devotion, and expressed love. Other things may burn and smoke, but they will not smell the same to God or man. Because worship is becoming popularized in the Church of Jesus Christ today, there is much religious nonsense being offered as incense unto God. But program cannot replace praise, and platform performance cannot replace congregational participation any more than orchestrated responses can substitute for spontaneous releases unto God. However popular it may have become, dramatization cannot replace realization of the Divine presence. We must be careful lest we offer to God an incense that is convenient to us but is not consistent with Him and His requirements.

There is undoubtedly a place in our churches for program, platform performance, drama, and an infinite variety of music forms, but if these are given as a substitute for worship rather than as a supplement to worship, what was intended as a fragrance may well become a stench to both God and His true worshippers. Korahs have to come up with substitutes because they have no access to that which is genuine, but true priests of worship have the correct incense available to them by Divine decree. The real may be discerned from the false by just a sensitive sniff of our spirits.

The most obvious problem in this test, of course, was that the wrong persons were offering the incense. God had reserved this activity for the Aaronic priesthood; Korah was but a Levite, and this company were usurper priests presuming to offer incense before God. Much later, when King Uzziah took it upon himself to offer incense in the Holy Place, God smote him with leprosy, and he remained a separated leper to his dying day (*see* 2 Chronicles 26:19), even though he was a good king, a godly king, and a king desperately needed by Israel.

How today's Christians need to learn that a person is not a worshipper because he worships; he worships because he is a worshipper. Who we are in God's sight determines what we do in His presence. Jesus told the woman at Jacob's well, " 'But the hour is coming, and now is, when **the true worshipers will worship the Father in spirit and truth'** " (John 4:23, emphasis added). Worshippers will worship, for that is consistent with their nature, but their activity did not produce their nature. Who we are sanctifies what we do. Korah and company were not content being who they were; they wanted to be who they were not, so nothing they did was acceptable, and they ended up being completely non-existent. Insistence upon having another's position in the Body of Christ not only causes an individual to forfeit his position, but usually results in his having no position whatever in the Church.

The basis of God's indictment against these malcontents was the burning of incense—worship. God did not have to say much; the false worship spoke volumes. Church politics may become complex, but when the incense of worship is finally offered, it does not take a national officer to ferret out the true from the false. God delights in letting us indict ourselves in the way we function in the role of a worshipping priest!

While the incense was still being wafted into the air, "the glory of the LORD appeared to all the congregation" (verse 19). In my wide traveling throughout the churches of the world, there have been occasions when I could have been taken in by things that were done as acts of worship. There are persons who use banners beautifully, others who dance almost profession-ally, and singers who sing most excellently, and my soul delights in these things and begins to rise to worship the Lord. But if the glory of the Lord comes in the midst of the people, it is easy to instantly tell that they do not know how to respond to the presence of the Lord. They have no relationship to the glory of God; their only relationship is to their own egos and their personal talents. The dividing line is the glory of God.

Some people who pray that the glory of the Lord might be manifested in their local congregations don't realize just how devastating this could be, for God's glory will always divide cleanly between the true and the false.

So they got away from around the tents of Korah, Dathan, and Abiram; and Dathan and Abiram came out and stood at the door of their tents, with their wives, their sons, and their little children. Then Moses said: "By this you shall know that the LORD has sent me to do all these works, for I have not done them of my own will. If these men die naturally like all men, or if they are visited by the common fate of all men, then the LORD has not sent me. But if the LORD creates a new thing, and the earth opens its mouth and swallows them up with all that belongs to them, and they go down alive into the pit, then you will understand that these men have rejected the LORD."

Then it came to pass, as he finished speaking all these words, that the ground split apart under them, and the earth opened its mouth and swallowed them up, with their households and all the men with Korah, with all their goods. So they and all those with them went down alive into the pit; the earth closed over them, and they perished from among the congregation.

Then all Israel who were around them fled at their cry, for they said, "Lest the earth swallow us up also!" And a fire came out from the LORD and consumed the two hundred and fifty men who were offering incense.

—(Numbers 16:27-35)

— 4 —

The Impact

God let these antagonists do their thing. Then He appeared! It is more than embarrassing when God shows up while we are "doing our thing"—it is deadly! The first thing that God did was to call for separation. " 'Separate yourselves from among this congregation, that I may consume them in a moment,' " God said (verse 21). Moses interceded with God for the people, but God merely said, " 'Speak to the congregation, saying, "Get away from the tents of Korah, Dathan, and Abiram" ' " (verse 24). The glory of the Lord always produces a separation between the true and the false.

Either Korah, Dathan, and Abiram did not join the 250 leaders and representatives of the congregation in the offering of the incense (which would not be too out of character, since the perpetrators of rebellions often push others to the forefront in times of confrontation), or they immediately went to their tents when the glory of the Lord appeared. Moses led the congregation to the tents of Dathan and Abiram and prophetically said, " 'By this you shall know that the LORD has sent me to do all these works, for I have not done them of my own will. If these men die naturally like all men, or if they are visited by the common fate of all men, then the LORD has not sent me. But if the LORD creates a new thing, and the earth opens its mouth and swallows them up with all that belongs to them, and they go down alive into the pit, then you will understand that these men have rejected the LORD' " (Numbers 16:28-30).

Hardly had Moses completed that statement when the earth opened and swallowed these three leaders of the rebellion. This was severe enough, but verses 32 and 33 declare that Dathan's and Abiram's wives, sons, and little children who stood with them in front of their tents also fell into the opened earth. It seems that "families that rebel together are judged together." It is not uncommon in a church to see an entire family take issue with the leadership at the same time, which has to testify that the parents have been discussing the issue in front of the children. From years of pastoral counseling I would challenge anyone that even if you are willing to risk God's judgment by rebelling against spiritual leadership, don't let your children in on it. Give them a chance to survive the death penalty you are asking for yourself.

This was swift and severe judgment by God. God more than revealed His definitive choice for the priesthood; He permanently removed the dissenters from Israel's congregation. Sometimes an exodus from a local church is God's "opened earth" to remove dissenters from the covenant people lest they lead those people into more rebellion. One of the first things my pastor father taught me about pastoring was "If people want to leave, let them go!" It may prevent a church split somewhere down the road to let God remove the dissatisfied before they become leaders of a mutiny.

New Testament Christians who have cut their spiritual teeth on the grace of God may find the severity of this judgment shocking, but doesn't this same New Testament warn us that "it is a fearful thing to fall into the hands of the living God" (Hebrews 10:31)? To contend with God's man is serious enough, but to contend with God over His choice of a man can have only destruction as its result. Korah craved the reins of leadership, but it got him and his cohorts a living burial while Israel watched.

In contrast to Dathan and Abiram, it appears that Korah stood alone; his family didn't join him in the revolt. As a matter of fact, Korah wasn't even standing in front of his tent when the earth opened up, for, as he was a Levite, his tent was in the area around the Tabernacle. He must have been standing with Dathan and Abiram by their tents. Korah stood apart from his family, and he died alone in his rebellion; his sons did not perish with him. When Israel's second census was taken, it was written, "These are the Dathan and Abiram, representatives of the congregation, who contended against Moses and Aaron in the company of Korah, when they contended against the LORD; and the earth opened its mouth and swallowed them up together with Korah when that company died, when the fire devoured two hundred and fifty men; and they became a sign. **Nevertheless the children of Korah did not die**" (Numbers 26:9-11, emphasis added).

Sovereign grace spared the sons of Korah from the fearful fate of their father. God did not visit the sins of the father upon the children. Later these sons of Korah, with their own sons, became the keepers of the gates of the Tabernacle. They had the cities of refuge. They were over the changers and the treasuries of the house of the Lord, and the instruments of the sanctuary—the wine, oil, etc.—were in their charge. They were mighty men of valor—strong men—who were made the royal guards for kings. Furthermore, the Holy Spirit inspired them to write some of the Psalms. Consider their background and the evident grace of God that had been extended to their lineage when you read Psalm 84, which is a psalm credited to the "sons of Korah":

> *How lovely is Your tabernacle, O LORD of hosts! My soul longs, yes, even faints for the courts of the LORD; my heart and my flesh cry out for the living God. I would rather be a doorkeeper in the house of my God than dwell in the tents of wickedness. For the LORD God is a sun and shield; the LORD will give grace and glory; no good thing will He withhold from those who walk uprightly (verses 1,2,10,11).*

The sons of Korah were spared the judgment of their father, and they served faithfully in the priesthood right up until the days of Jesus. Had that entire family been involved in the rebellion of Korah, we would have lost much ministry that was needed in the Body of Christ. Sometimes rebellion in the Church produces the same effects as abortion in natural life. A needed future generation is destroyed before we have a chance to see what they could have contributed. How many Christian statesmen, pastors, theologians, missionaries, translators, and lay workers have been lost to us simply because their families involved them in a rebellion against God's leadership when they were children? What a waste!

But the leaders with their families were not the only ones destroyed in God's chastisements. Verse 35 tells us that the 250 "leaders, representatives, men of renown" were consumed in the fire that came out from the Lord. What an impact this would have on Israel! Have you ever imagined what an irreparable loss to Israel this was? Try to conceive of the loss of the pastoring staff, elders, deacons, Sunday School workers, and musicians of a large church—all in a single day. Only the pastor and assistant (Moses and Aaron) remained out of all of Israel's leaders. They had not been out of Egypt very long. They needed their leaders, but the leaders wanted more authority than God had ordained for them, and they were killed by the action of God, leaving Israel short 253 leaders.

How the Body of Christ has suffered when key leadership has been set aside by God for rebelling against His ways and His man. Churches that once had trusted leaders and workers and servants have often suffered irreparable damage when these leaders were chastened by God for rebellion. I have seen churches of several thousand members close their doors when the leadership was set aside because of sin. Sheep without a shepherd are quickly scattered and become the prey of wolves and other predators.

When leaders are lost, it is difficult to replace them, for leadership arises by capacity, and it takes time to develop that capacity. A hastily summoned business meeting could fill the vacancy with bodies, but both God and pastors often spend years preparing a true leader. Also, there are abilities, traits, and characteristics that are innate within good leaders. Any time you remove 250 key leaders from a congregation, that congregation is going to suffer. The impact of this judgment upon Israel will never be fully understood by us, but one wonders if the constant murmuring of Israel in the years that followed might have been averted if these rebelling leaders had been content to work with Moses on the team instead of working against him in hopes of replacing him.

This fire that went out from the Lord and destroyed the 250

leaders of Israel also consumed everything that pertained to their rebellion. Their censers, now blackened from the heat of the Divine fire, were gathered at God's command, "and they were hammered out as a covering on the altar, to be a memorial to the children of Israel that no outsider, who is not a descendant of Aaron, should come near to offer incense before the LORD" (verses 39,40). These men were Outer Court ministers trying to become Inner Court men, and so, after slaying them, God placed their implements of worship where they belonged—in the Outer Court, for God does not mix bronze and gold, and worship is a golden activity. These censers that had been used as instruments of rebellion against God were made into a covering for the Brazen Altar, just as all weapons that have been formed against Christ eventually hang on His cross as trophies of His conquest.

Still another impact of God's judgment upon this revolt was that the Divine fire consumed the false fire. When the Divine fire went out from God and consumed the men, it also consumed everything they had in their censers. When God's fire arrives, it destroys everything that the false fire feeds upon; and, as Proverbs teaches us, when the wood is consumed the fire goes out (*see* Proverbs 26:20). God's presence can consume more wood in one hour than rebellion can consume in a year. I've watched the fire of the presence of God purge the pride, rebellion, self-centeredness, and sin from the hearts of an entire congregation in one service. It is not by accident that Hebrews 12:29 declares, "Our God is a consuming fire." None of us will ever be able to kindle a blaze that can stand in the presence of our God.

It is still a reality that where there is true worship, the false is destroyed. The best answer to "wildfire" is the real fire! God's presence consumes the fire in wrong censers. As surely as the best answer to the demonic is the Divine, the safest answer to the false is the true, and only God Himself is the True Fire upon which our incense may be sprinkled.

The wrong incense of these impostor priests would also have been completely destroyed in this fire of God's presence, for incense is released by a coal of fire but is destroyed by a flame of fire, and God appeared as a flame of fire right out of the pillar of fire that rested over the Holy of Holies. The mockery of these men's false worship was forever removed by the majesty of God's presence in the form of fire.

Then the LORD spoke to Moses, saying: "Tell Eleazar, the son of Aaron the priest, to pick up the censers out of the blaze, for they are holy, and scatter the fire some distance away. The censers of these men who sinned aginst their own souls, let them be made into hammered plates as a covering for the altar. Because they presented them before the LORD, therefore they are holy; and they shall be a sign to the children of Israel."

So Eleazar the priest took the bronze censers, which those who were burned up had presented, and they were hammered out as a covering on the altar, to be a memorial to the children of Israel that no outsider, who is not a descendant of Aaron, should come near to offer incense before the LORD, that he might not become like Korah and his companions, just at the LORD had said to him through Moses.

—(Numbers 16:36-40)

— 5 —

The Insubordination

That demonstration is not always a deterrent is graphically illustrated in the story told in Numbers 16. Even though the entire congregation of Israel had witnessed the chastening hand of God upon their leaders, after sleeping on the painful memory of the cleaving of the earth and the lightning-like flame that flashed furiously from the pillar of fire from over the Tabernacle, "all the congregation of the children of Israel murmured against Moses and Aaron, saying, 'You have killed the people of the LORD' " (verse 41). Seeing the penalty for rebellion did not prevent their continued rebellion. If rebellion involves a driving spirit force, no amount of physical punishment will conquer this spirit of witchcraft that desires to take control, for spirit forces are not controlled by physical means.

"You have killed the people of the Lord," the congregation chanted. Emotional outbursts prevent sound reasoning, and no one would deny that the preceding day had been an extremely emotional one. Their forensic coup de main had been met with Divine weapons so fearsome as to boggle their minds and churn their emotions to a fever pitch. The long night of grief over the loss of loved ones, relatives, and friends had reached the anger stage, and that anger was vented against Moses as they charged him with the responsibility for the deaths of the 253 rebel leaders.

Because Moses, as a prophet, proclaimed in advance what God was about to do, the people blamed Moses for God's chastisement. It is still all too common to see the proclaimer as the producer and to blame the prophet for the fulfilled prophecy. In the days of absolute monarchies, messengers dreaded taking bad news to the king, for it was quite ordinary for the king to order the execution of a bearer of bad tidings, as though the messenger were responsible for the news he carried. Similarly, Jesus reminded the Jews of His day, " 'Therefore you are witnesses against yourselves that you are sons of those who murdered the prophets' " (Matthew 24:31). God mercifully sent messengers with warnings, but Israel killed the messengers rather than heed the warnings. Human nature does not change unless it submits to the Divine nature of God as made available to us at Calvary. We still blame the leader for God's actions.

In spite of God's many demonstrations of His choice of Moses to lead Israel in the wilderness, the people remained unafraid to murmur against him. How strong is the spirit of independence in all of us! With only a portion of the facts at hand, we seek to overrule the authority of those who have both natural and spiritual information with which to make a judgment.

Moses must have stood incredulous while these fresh charges were being levied against him, but in the midst of the murmuring of the people, God's glory appeared (*see* verse 42). While we usually associate a demonstration of the glory of God with a fervent prayer meeting or a time of high-level worship, Israel was beginning to get accustomed to a demonstration of the glory of God in the midst of her rebellion, for just one day earlier the glory of God had preceded the Divine burial of Dathan, Abiram, and Korah and the incineration of the 250 elders and deacons of Israel. God's glory symbolizes His manifested presence, and what proceeds out of that "cloud of great glory," as we like to sing, is not always pleasant to the flesh.

The moment the glory appeared, Moses and Aaron left the complaining congregation and went into the Holy Place to commune with God, for God's presence is always the safest place for a leader to be when he is in the midst of murmuring and rebellion. It is far more profitable to talk to God than to dispute with antagonists. In appearing to Israel in the cloud of His presence, God accepted the charges as being against Him rather than against Moses. How difficult it is to fight against God's leader without actually fighting against God Himself. A clever church board may successfully unseat a pastor, but they will discover that they are issuing a challenge to Almighty God, and He is a fierce foe. He not only has weapons unavailable to us; He has all eternity on His side, while men must contend with Him amidst the limited days of their sojourn on this earth.

Standing before God in the Holy Place, Moses and Aaron were shocked to hear God command them, " 'Get away from among this congregation, that I may consume them in a moment' " (verse 45). Both of these rejected leaders fell prostrate before the Lord, and even as they waited in God's presence, a plague from the Lord began to move among the people. "All the congregation" had joined Korah in his rebellious cry (verse 19). "All the congregation" united to blame Moses for the deaths (verse 41), so now "all the congregation" were about to share in Korah's death.

It may seem to be a light thing to encourage a person in his rebellion against God's leadership, but when the judgment of God comes, all who are participants in that rebellion share equally in God's wrath. The difference in this story is that the leaders knew what they were doing. It was a definite power play to take over the leadership. The people, however, knew only what they were being told by these men and were acting out of loyalty to their leaders and the cry of "equality to all." The perpetrators of the insurrection were judged immediately, but those who had walked with them in their stand against Aaron were given twelve to twenty-four hours to rethink their actions in the light of God's response, to repent, and to change their hearts. But they didn't. They only became more adamant in their cry of "Moses, you're a harsh, cruel tyrant who stays in office by killing all who oppose you."

Just as God responded to Jezebel and her followers in the Church in Thyatira by saying, " 'I gave her time to repent . . . and she did not repent. Indeed I will cast her into a sickbed, and those who commit adultery with her into great tribulation, unless they repent of their deeds' " (Revelation 2:21,22), so God responded to His sinning people in the midst of this insurrection against leadership. God gave them a space to repent—even though it was only one night, it was still a "grace period"—but their frustration only simmered into greater indignation against Moses. God had vindicated Aaron in the matter of the incense, but Moses was still a target for their attack.

This time there was no test or chance to substantiate their charges. A plague came out from the presence of the Lord as silently as the death plague that had killed Egypt's firstborn sons. Could this have been the same plague? While God had promised that He would not inflict any of the plagues He had put upon the Egyptians, He did so with the provision " 'if you diligently heed the voice of the LORD your God and do what is right in His sight, give ear to His commandments and keep all His statutes' " (Exodus 15:26). Therefore this present uprising against both the ecclesiastical and the civil leadership that God had installed over them canceled their exemption, for covenants (or·contracts) demand compliance by all parties to that covenant in order to remain valid. The very moment Israel ceased to obey God and follow His commands and His leadership, they canceled His covenant, and within a few hours the death plague to which they had been previously granted immunity was destroying them. Only this time it was not merely the firstborn sons; no one seemed to be exempted from this outburst of God's plague. They may have believed that they were merely challenging aging leadership, but, as God later said, " '. . . take note, you have sinned against the LORD, and be sure your sin will find you out' " (Numbers 32:23).

We are never in deeper trouble than when we try to tell God that He is doing wrong. When we seek to substitute our provision for God's provision, especially in the matter of leadership, we have put ourselves in opposition to God.

Neither Moses nor Israel could say of the chastisements or plague that accident or chance brought them upon the nation. God forced them to admit, "It is the Lord." There are times when God must force us to admit, "It is the Lord," because all of us are prone to rationalize the supernatural out of the natural events of our lives and declare them to be fate, chance, happenstance, etc. We need to guard our lives lest our Western culture's penchant for science and education so removes us from the teaching of the Word that we forget that God says,

" 'As many as I love, I rebuke and chasten' " (Revelation 3:19). If we Americans have done as the Israelites did, we will be treated as they were treated, for God was chastening His sons back to obedience.

There is still a God Who judges in this world. Were He to allow us to censure any of His ways, it would frustrate His purposes, rob Him of His honor, and lower Him in the eyes of saints and sinners alike. For the sake of His character and reputation among men, God will not allow rebels to overthrow His rulership on earth, even when that reign is exercised through human agents.

This action of the congregation of Israel evidenced an utter contempt for God's warnings. A full twenty-four hours had not passed since the earth had opened in judgment and flaming fire had cremated their leaders, and yet the people were still crying, "We have a right to make decisions; we have a right to choose our leaders; we are equal to Aaron in the priesthood and to Moses in civil leadership." They just hadn't learned the lessons that God had sought to teach them the day before. While experience is a good teacher, it can also be a deadly teacher. Yesterday several hundred leaders had learned "Don't tell God what He can do," but they were never able to use that information, because by the time they learned it they were already dying. Now the living were refusing to learn from the dead and were exposing themselves to the wrath of God by ignoring God's ways and warnings. If we refuse to learn by observation, then we must learn by experience.

Moses and Aaron were in the Holy Place, prostrate before the Almighty in the Shekinah of God, when the plague broke out. In the case of the opened earth, Moses was given prior knowledge of God's acts, but in the case of this plague, Moses discovered it only after it had begun. Intercession demands involvement with God. Prior knowledge of His actions permits the intercessor to do something in advance. On repeated occasions God told Moses what He intended to do to Israel, and Moses was able to intercede with Him before the fact, thereby preventing His action. But in this case it seems that God said, "I know what you'll do, Moses. You'll intercede to talk Me out of My actions, so I'll just call you into My presence to enjoy fellowship with Me while I chasten My rebellious children outside."

But Moses had developed an inner sensitivity to God during the many days he had spent in God's presence on Mount Sinai. He not only felt the joy of God's glory in the Holy Place; he was able to sense the plague of death going out from the presence of God into the midst of Israel's camp. Because Moses knew his God, he expected both mercy and judgment. " '. . . the people who know their God shall be strong and carry out great exploits' " (Daniel 11:32) was God's later affirmation to Daniel.

There are times when we desperately need to know more than what God is doing and saying. We need to know God, for He works according to His nature and will, and only an understanding of that nature and will enables us to be involved with Him before His actions are demonstrated. We do not need to have great knowledge of God to know what God is saying if He is saying it publicly, but if God chooses to withhold communicated knowledge and yet we know the heart of God, there will be an intuitive or spiritual understanding that gives us knowledge out of relationship with God, not too unlike the understanding that develops between a husband and wife who have lived in a loving relationship for many years.

God does not always forewarn His people of specific actions, but He always invites us into His presence during times of judgment, and in that presence there often comes a spiritual knowing of the ways of the Lord. Too often the modern Church seems to be playing "catch-up" in Her ministry of intercession because Her relationship with God is out of date. This forces the Church to deal with God about what He has done, not what He is doing, much less be able to intercede with Him about what He is going to do.

Hundreds of years after this incident, David wrote, "He made known His ways to Moses, His acts to the children of Israel" (Psalm 103:7). A distinguishing difference between Moses and the children of Israel is that Moses knew God's ways, which enabled him to know what God was going to do before He did it, but the congregation knew only God's acts. Obviously, if we know only God's acts we will know only where God has been and what He has done. If we know only the acts of God, we will forever live in the past. It's time for the Church to know more than what God did. We need to know Who God is! We need to emulate Paul, who cried, "That I may know Him . . ." (Philippians 3:10).

Moses may not have known that the plague was coming, but he well knew the God Who was sending that plague. He ignored God's action and responded to His Person, somewhat like the mother of Jesus at the wedding at Cana, who, in spite of Christ's gentle rebuff, told the servants, " 'Whatever He says to you, do it' " (John 2:5). There are times when we, too, should be mature enough in our relationship with God that we dare ignore what seem to be the actions of God and respond to the Person of God.

No one would dare enter the Holy Place to tell Moses about the death-dealing plague. Moses' knowledge had to come from a spiritual intuitiveness, but even with this knowledge he also knew how hampered he was in dealing with it. He had to resort to a different method of intercession to appease God's wrath, since all other means were by now exhausted. For instance, he couldn't stake his life for the nation, as he had done at Horeb (*see* Exodus 32:32), for the nation had just rejected him as their leader. Their rejection left him without a bargaining position with God. He could no longer appeal to the honor of Jehovah among the heathen, seeing that the Lord had assured him that the whole earth—not merely the nation of Israel—should be filled with the glory of God. He couldn't even pray that God would not be wrathful with all the nation for the sake of one or a few sinners, as he had done the day before (*see* verse 22), since the whole congregation had now joined in revolt against him.

So Moses had to reach for some fresh means of intercession. It seems that Israel's deliverance became dependent upon someone other than Moses; it became dependent upon the exercise of the ministry of the high priest, against whom yesterday's revolution had been aimed. It wasn't the last time God would choose to minister through one the people had rejected. It was as though God said, "You want to put him down? I'll raise him up and use him as My means of delivering you." If we get too choosy about whom God uses to rescue us we will probably perish in the plague, for God does not give up on His man just because the people have rejected him.

It was a demonstration of God's mercy that Aaron was chosen to be the intercessor who stood between the people and God's righteous wrath. Nothing could reinstate him into the hearts of the people faster than seeing him as their source of life. But it was also a demonstration of merciful kindness on Aaron's part, for the congregation had risen up in rebellion against him. Certainly it would have been satisfying to Aaron's carnal nature to have remained in God's holy presence, as a good priest was supposed to do, and worship God while the Divine wrath was destroying all who had insurrected against him. But instead it seems that God was saying, "Aaron, if you'll forgive them, I'll forgive them. If you will go back out among the people, I will go with you. If you will intreat for them, I will be intreated of you for them." Possibly God's mercy in sparing Aaron when he joined Miriam in insurrection against Moses gave Aaron extra grace and mercy in interceding for the congregation, for while God had smitten Miriam, He had spared Aaron. It seems to follow that those who have received mercy are quicker to extend mercy. When Satan trips a leader, plunging him into the mud of sin, he thinks he has destroyed that person's usefulness, but often God turns it to His own glory and so imparts grace to the fallen one that all future ministry is seasoned with grace and mercy far beyond the ministry level before the fall. Aaron had received great grace, and now in mercy he was extending it to others.

We can also see beautiful submission in Aaron, for he, and he alone, could intercede successfully for the people on this occasion, and yet he sweetly took instruction from Moses in all the details of his activity. Having served as high priest for several months, he undoubtedly knew everything that Moses was telling him about choosing the censer, getting the fire, and carrying the incense separately; yet even though he had now become the number one intercessor, he realized that this did not make him the number one leader. Frankly, intercessors aren't leaders; they are intercessors. Unfortunately, some intercessors have taken authority above a local pastor by reporting to him, "In our prayer time, God spoke, and this is wrong, and that is wrong, and this is what you have to do." This is not too unlike some apostolic groups who claim to honor their apostles as their ultimate leaders, but the prophets tell the apostles what to do. The apostles have titular headship, but the prophets have practical headship. I have ministered in some places where the intercessors have become the leaders of the leader when they shouldn't have been dealing with the leadership at all, but with God.

Aaron was admirably submitted to the leadership of Moses, his brother, but he was equally courageous in carrying out that will. First of all, running out among those who want to kill you is evidence of either courage or stupidity, and then going out in the midst of a killer plague took courage. How easily he could have rationalized his great importance to Israel as her only high priest, and stayed in the protective presence of Almighty God. But rather than isolate himself from, and insulate himself against, the plague, he ran right into the midst of it for the sake of the dying people. What zeal this aged man demonstrated not only in going out among the plagued people but in actually running out among them (*see* verse 47). Their only hope rested in him, and he rushed among them to stay the judgment of God. God give us more pastors who are zealous for the people even in the midst of rebellion and strife!

In his *Commentary on the Old Testament*, Volume 1, Keil says that the plague was a sudden death. It was not a sickness that led to death; death was almost instantaneous. The scriptural account says that "Aaron stood between the dead and the living; so the plague was stopped" (verse 48). In *The Targum of Jonathan* this verse is translated "He stood in prayer in the middle, and made a partition, with his censer, between the dead and the living." This plague of sudden death proceeded no further than where Aaron stood to offer his incense as an atonement to God.

Carrying the sacred fire and the Divinely-formulated incense into the midst of the infected people, Aaron became the means of their deliverance. As he waved his censer and its fumes went up to heaven, faith in Jehovah and in Aaron as the true priest of Jehovah was revived in men's hearts. The incense that yesterday was so common that rebels would dare to offer it, now revived their spirits to believe that He Who smites also heals, and He Who kills also makes alive.

The smoking incense here probably has a significance similar to the brazen serpent later (chapter 21). That was another occasion of rebellion, and God sent fiery serpents among the people to kill them. When Moses interceded on behalf of the people, God instructed him to cast a bronze serpent in the form of the destroying snakes and to raise it on a pole in the midst of the camp. The people were told that if they would come and gaze upon this serpent, they would survive the serpents' bites. As has so often been preached, it was "Look and live!"

We are certainly aware that looking at bronze replicas does not cure snakebite. It was the obedience of accepting God's provision both in their spirits and by their action of looking that brought the healing of Jehovah into their lives.

On that occasion it was visual stimulation that stirred faith; here it was olfactory stimulation. Those who had been smelling the death plague while hearing the screams of those who were dying as well as of those who were terrorized by people dying around them, now smell something different. Incense! Aaron had come among them with the incense of God. The incense took their minds off the judgment of God and focused their thoughts on the God of the judgment, and when that happened, the plague was stayed. Whereas at the one occurrence we have the message of "Look and live," here we have the truth "Smell and live."

Aaron was, of course, a type of our Great High Priest, Jesus

Christ, Who rushed into our encampment at Bethlehem of Judea to waft the incense of worship of the Father in the midst of a people who were being destroyed by the plague of sin.

One day earlier, the 250 censers of the rebels had effected nothing but death, but this day the one censer of the true high priest saved the lives of millions of people. Aaron's incense made an atonement in the midst of rebellion, but his incense was restrictive, not remedial. It only gave the living who were capable of smelling the incense a chance to continue living. It "stood between"; it did not resurrect, for intercession does not reach beyond the living. There is no scriptural evidence that even our Great High Priest, Jesus Christ, makes intercession for the dead. It is for the living that Christ intercedes; once the judgment of God descends, there is no provision for repentance and restoration on the other side of the grave.

Still, if Aaron, with his censer and incense, could disarm the wrath of an insulted, angry God so that a guilty people who deserved nothing but destruction should be spared, how much more effectual is Christ's great atonement! While the sacrifices of living animals pointed to the death of Christ on the cross, the incense points to Christ's continued intercession for us, since "He is also able to save to the uttermost those who come to God through Him, since He ever lives to make intercession for them" (Hebrews 7:25).

On the next day all the congregation of the children of Israel murmured against Moses and Aaron, saying, "You have killed the people of the LORD."

Now it happened, when the congregation had gathered against Moses and Aaron, that they turned toward the tabernacle of meeting; and suddenly the cloud covered it, and the glory of the LORD appeared.

Then Moses and Aaron came before the tabernacle of meeting. And the LORD spoke to Moses, saying, "Get away from among this congregation, that I may consume them in a moment." And they fell on their faces, So Moses said to Aaron, "Take a censer and put fire in it from the altar, put incense on it, and take it quickly to the congregation and make atonement for them; for wrath has gone out from the LORD. The plague has begun."

Then Aaron took it as Moses commanded, and ran into the midst of the congregation; and already the plague had begun among the people. So he put in the incense and made atonement for the people. And he stood between the dead and the living; so the plague was stopped. Now those who died in the plague were fourteen thousand seven hundred, besides those who died in the Korah incident. So Aaron returned to Moses at the door of the tabernacle of meeting, for the plague had stopped.

—(Numbers 16:41-50)

— 6 —

The Atonement

Just as Aaron exemplified, the proper **response** to rebellion around us is **worship**. All churches are subject to rebellion and insurrection, whether it be an occasional Miriam and Aaron or a general uprising under a Korah. The past few years in my traveling ministry I have witnessed an increasing amount of rebellion in the churches of America. The size of the church, its doctrinal emphasis, or its form of expression have little to do with rebellion. I find it among staff members, in elderships, in church boards, and even among home-group leaders. Rebellion is always rooted in pride, never in principle. If the issue were actually a principle, there are channels through which it can be handled.

Generally the small measure of principle that is proclaimed as an issue is little more than a smokescreen to cover the action of a little person trying to get someone else's position. His premise is built upon a partial truth that sounds correct, and the spirit force behind the rebellion makes it very enticing to the flesh, but, of course, in seeking to dethrone earthly leaders in the Church, we risk rising up against God and sharing Korah's fate.

Sometimes we unwittingly get involved by thinking that we can "straighten out" the thinking of the rebels, but by the time they have contacted us, it is too late to straighten them out. We are but numbers on their petitions. Rebels view us as cannon fodder for their fight. They didn't bother contacting us until they needed a group to stand up and be counted as the "loyal opposition." The more we listen to them, the more we will be contaminated by them. We need to hang up the phone and get back to worshipping God.

When Korahs rise among us, suggesting that we replace the present leadership with themselves, our best response is to ignore them and worship God, for we cannot rejoice and worship God while entangled in mutiny any more than we can be involved in an insurrection and flow in worship unto God. Worship will form a dividing line. We can keep our own spirits clean if we will worship instead of criticize.

"But," you may counter, "there are some things that are not right." That may depend upon what you call right and wrong. There will often be things that are not being done your way, and I may see things that are not being done my way, but frankly, that doesn't make either one of us right or wrong. Different is neither inferior nor wrong; it is merely different. Of course, if it is a clear violation of accepted teaching of Scripture, then we should make our approach through proper channels to have the situation corrected, and if this does not settle the situation, we should probably gently move on to a church situation where we can be comfortable. Is there an issue large enough to justify splitting a church over it?

Not only is worship the **response** to rebellion; it is the **solution** to rebellion around us. In the rebellion of Korah, God let worship be the dividing line between the called ones and the usurpers. It was the use of incense that discerned between the true and the false. Discipline and confrontation rarely stop church rebellion, but worship does. If God cannot defend His Church, then it is not worth defending, but God will not defend it if we are trying to defend it. We can deal either with the insurrectionists or with God. When rebels are challenged to worship God with the God-appointed leadership, lines are immediately drawn. If the rebel worships in spirit and truth, his rebellion will be broken, but if he fakes worship, God will deal severely with him.

We can encourage ourselves in the knowledge that the action of a rebel never destroys reality. When Korah's rebellion and the insurrection of the people were finally settled by God, what was left was what God had originally appointed: a priesthood, a sacrificial system, and a channel of communication with Himself through the burning of incense. The only change was that the rebels had been purged from the congregation, and it takes purification of the Church to maintain pure worship of God. When the Church is flowing in the pure incense of worship, it will have a healing effect upon rebellion and an atoning action against the plague of God's judgment.

Thank God for Aaron, Israel's high priest, by whose intercession Israel was spared the certain death she deserved because of her insistent rejection of God's leaders. Thank God, too, for Christ Jesus, our Great High Priest, by whose continual intercession we are daily spared the certain death that we deserve for turning "every one, to his own way" (Isaiah 53:6). Without the High Priestly ministry of Jesus, none of us would make it into heaven, even after our conversion, for Israel was a covenant people by God's choosing, just as the Church is in our generation.

As a matter of fact, the book of Hebrews is built around the High Priestly ministry of Christ. A dozen or more times in that book He is called our High Priest, and He is alluded to as our High Priest on other occasions. In the eighth chapter, however, we are given a view of Him that is somewhat unique. At first it is declared, "We have such a High Priest, who is seated at the right hand of the throne of the Majesty in the heavens," but three verses later we read, "For if He were on earth, He would not be a priest, since there are priests who offer the gifts according to the law" (Hebrews 8:1,4).

The emphasis here is not so much a suggestion that He would be rejected on earth as a priest as it is an emphasis on His High Priestly function in the Holy Place. There are other priests who are ordained of God to function on Christ's behalf on the earth. Twice the final book of the Bible declares that Christ Jesus has made us to be "kings and priests unto God," or, as some translators handle the Greek, "a kingdom of priests" (Revelation 1:6, 5:10), and even Peter described us as a "royal priesthood" (1 Peter 2:9).

At His resurrection, Christ accepted the limitations of a human body for all eternity. Even though it is the glorified body that we shall wear throughout eternity, it is nonetheless a body that localizes the spirit. As Christ Jesus in the heavens, He is spoken of as seated on the Throne of God and functioning as the Head of His earthly Body, which is the Church. Paul became bold enough to declare, "For we are members of His body, of His flesh and of His bones." ". . . in whom you also are being built together for a habitation of God in the Spirit." "Now you are the body of Christ, and members individually" (Ephesians 5:30, 2:22; 1 Corinthians 12:27). Immediately after declaring the Church to be Christ's functioning Body on earth, Paul spoke of God's appointment of apostles, prophets, teachers, miracles, gifts of healings, helps, administrations, etc., showing the variety of functions that can be expected in this earthly, but spiritual, Body of Christ. Mystical? Yes! But it is extremely practical at the same time.

God has provided a functioning Body for Christ on the earth in the multi-membered Church. The orders come from the Head, but they are executed through the members of the Body on earth. We are interdependent upon one another. As surely as "without Him I can do nothing," without us He will do nothing here on the earth, for He has purposed to work through His human agencies who represent Him on earth.

In light of this, could the action of Aaron in taking the incense of the Holy Place out among the judged congregation be a picture of believer-priests functioning among men today? Consistently the Bible teaches that unrepentant men are dead in trespasses and sins. What killed them? —the plague of sin! This plague affects "all the congregation" of the world. Explorers have never discovered a single tribe or village with a sinless population. Sin is universal. "All have sinned and fall short of the glory of God" (Romans 3:23).

God needs an "Aaron" here on the earth to stand between the destroying plague and living persons. Rebellious men will perish unless someone makes them aware of a saving atonement, for although all men know sin, multitudes of persons have no knowledge of a saving God, since no one has brought them a lingering scent of the incense of God. Just as Aaron did not burn the incense in the Holy Place before the presence of God on this occasion, but burned it among the people in the midst of the plague, even so believer-priests need to take the fragrance of the knowledge of God into the midst of the killing plague of sin in this world.

When Moses instructed Aaron to take this incense out to the people, he added, " '. . . take it quickly to the congregation and make atonement for them; for wrath has gone out from the LORD' " (verse 46). In recounting Aaron's obedience, the Bible says, "So he put in the incense and made atonement for the people" (verse 47). Aaron made an atonement simply by burning incense among the people!

Atonement by incense? Theologically, most of us have been taught that atonement comes by blood. What a surprising remedy this is. What physician would prescribe this as a cure for the plague? No theologian would recommend the burning of incense to stay the hand of God in the time of judgment, but Paul reminded us that "God has chosen the foolish things of the world to put to shame the wise, and God has chosen the weak things of the world to put to shame the things which are mighty; and the base things of the world and the things which are despised God has chosen, and the things which are not, to bring to nothing the things that are, that no flesh should glory in His presence" (1 Corinthians 1:27-29). So if God was pleased to have an atonement made with incense rather than sacrifice, we simply bow to His sovereignty.

It might help our understanding to know that the word translated here as "atonement" is *kaphar*, which literally means "to cover"—hence, to expiate, cancel, or placate. The English word "atonement" is not a translation of *kaphar*; it is actually a translator's *interpretation*. The only time the English word "atonement" is used in the King James Version of the Bible is in Romans 3:25; the New King James Version translated this Greek word *katallage* as "reconciliation," for the word "atonement" does not correspond etymologically with any Hebrew or Greek word which it translates. Nothing that was ever done by the priesthood of the Old Testament produced an "at-one-ment" with God. It produced an appeasement or a propitiation. The sacrifices of the Old Testament provided ritualistic confession of sin, and God "covered," or, as Paul put it, "God passed over the sins that were previously committed" (Romans 3:25), but even if they had slaughtered thousands upon thousands of animals as a propitiation of God, it would never have brought the people into an "at-one-ment" with God. That was the heartbroken cry of God through the prophets: "You keep your rituals current, but your heart is far from Me."

No, the holocaust sacrifices of the Old Testament did not bring man and God together; they merely covered man's sin with the sprinkled blood, and, as at the institution of the Passover, " 'when He sees the blood on the lintel and on the two doorposts, the LORD will pass over the door and not allow the destroyer to come into your houses to strike you' " (Exodus 12:23). The sin had not been settled, but it had been covered with God's provision, and by this act of obedience man secured exemption from God's wrath. The sin was covered, but it was still present in all of its putrefaction. Like garbage put in the trash can, it was out of sight, but the longer it remains in the can, the worse it stinks.

These sacrifices of the Old Testament did not replace, preempt, or prevent Christ's great sacrifice at Calvary; they merely covered the sins in anticipation of that coming sacrifice Who actually " 'takes away the sin of the world!' " (John 1:29). Only Jesus Christ can bring us into an "at-one-ment" with God, and this work, which begins at the cross, continues in the life of the believer through the sanctification of the Holy Spirit. The Spirit progressively brings us from our own ways into God's ways, from our world into God's world. Paul spoke of this as learning to "walk in the Spirit . . . live in the Spirit . . . be led by the Spirit" (*see* Galatians 5:14-25). This brings us into a harmonious relationship with God.

While none of the Old Testament rituals could get man and God together, they did make provision to cover all the sins of the covenant people until God became man and redeemed man from sin once and for all. Therefore, Aaron's incense did not bring the people into a fresh union with God; it formed a cloud that acted as a covering for the people until a change of heart could produce a confession of sin and the offering of a sacrifice.

In all atonement, or reconciliation, in both the Old and New Testaments, the initiative is of God, Who not only devises and reveals the way to reconciliation but, by means of angels, prophets, priests, and ultimately His only begotten Son, applies the means of atonement and persuades men to accept the conciliation that God has offered. So since propitiation is totally God's provision, He has a right to do it by blood, by brazen serpent, or by the offering of incense. And on this occasion He said, " 'Take incense and make an atonement for them' " (verse 46). Perhaps He was suggesting, "Turn their minds toward Me, and I will turn My mind from their sins."

Is it possible that in this day and age God is raising up believer-priests to preach worship, practice worship, sing worship, and demonstrate worship to form an incense cloud in the world? Is this the reason some have been inspired to write books about praise and worship, and others, to travel throughout the world conducting praise and worship seminars? Could this explain why, in almost every geographic district of the United States, God seems to have raised up at least one worshipping church? Are these performing the same act as Aaron by burning the incense of worship that can waft out into the community and make atonement for our generation? It doesn't change their rebellion or what they deserve because of that rebellion, but it changes God's action. God, Who skipped over the homes sprinkled with blood, saying, "When I see the blood, I will pass over you," also said by action, "When I see the brazen serpent, I will pass over you," and "When I see and smell the incense, I will pass over you."

It seems that God is teaching some of His covenant people to worship, to be censer-carriers, and to burn incense right in the midst of the plague of sin in order to delay the judgment of God. The prophets among us are declaring the impending judgment of God upon America, and we certainly deserve it. But who can tell if the plague God has purposed may be delayed or prevented entirely if more believer-priests, as representatives of our Great High Priest in heaven, will fill their lives with worship and go among the inhabitants of the land, creating a God-consciousness among the people?

Pure worship of God can make a difference in the working of the plague of God's judgment upon sin. This is both illustrated here in the sixteenth chapter of Numbers and declared in Second Corinthians, where Paul wrote, "Now thanks be to God who always leads us in triumph in Christ, and through us diffuses the fragrance of His knowledge in every place. For we are to God the fragrance of Christ among those who are being saved and among those who are perishing. To the one we are the aroma of death to death, and to the other the aroma of life to life. And who is sufficient for these things?" (2 Corinthians 2:14-16). Conybeare translates this, "And by me sends forth the knowledge of Him, a stream of fragrant incense, throughout the world. For Christ's is the fragrance which I offer up to God, whether among those in the way of salvation; or among those in the way of perdition; but to these it is an odour of death, to those of life."

Here Paul was alluding to the Roman "Triumphant," which was the highest honor bestowed upon a victorious general in ancient Rome. To be awarded a "triumph," a man must have been a magistrate holding supreme and independent command, and must have won a major land or sea battle. The Senate both granted and paid for the honor. It opened with a solemn procession from the Campus Martius to the Capitol, through streets adorned with garlands and lined with people shouting, "Io triumphe." At the head of the parade marched the magistrates and the Senate, followed by trumpeters; then came the spoils (arms, standards, statues, etc.), sacrificial animals, and captured prisoners. These prisoners were shackled together and carried censers of incense in their hands.

The victorious general, riding in a chariot adorned with laurel, wore the royal purple tunic and toga and held a laurel or palm branch in his right hand and an ivory scepter in his left hand. Behind him marched his conquering soldiers, singing anything they liked. Upon reaching the Capitoline temple, the general presented his laurel, along with thank offerings, to the image of Jupiter, and then everyone marched to the arena. There many of the prisoners were put to death in entertaining games to show the power of this victor over the lives of his enemies; some were freed to demonstrate the mercy of this honored general.

Paul saw himself a captive of Christ, Who conquered him on the road to Damascus and put him—and us—in the triumphal procession that God and heaven voted for Jesus. At the front of the parade are the Living Creatures and Elders of heaven, followed by the many trophies of Christ's conquests, and then those of us who have been captured by grace, waving our censers of incense. Then comes the triumphant Christ, riding in the victorious chariot and followed by the heavenly host, who have never lost any battle into which Christ led them, singing such songs as only those in the heavens can sing.

Paul seemed to sense that the incense burned by the prisoners, and that offered along the parade route, had an amazing symbolism of life and death. To those prisoners who had advance knowledge that they were to be released, the fragrance was a sweet odor of life. They could tell themselves that it was just a few more miles of marching, and then they would be free to return home to friends and loved ones. "The general may have the triumph, but I have life" was what the incense said to them.

But those who knew that they had been separated by the casting of lots to die in public sport at the arena walked with a dragging step. Every time they sniffed the incense, it was an odor of death. "This is ignominy. I'm a trained soldier. Why must I be killed just to demonstrate the power and authority of this general?" they were thinking.

Paul suggested that our very lives become a fragrance of life to those who are living and a smell of death to those who are dying in sin. Our skin, hair, and clothes have become so saturated with the incense we have been offering along the parade route that we give the knowledge of life and death.

Since God diffuses the fragrance of Christ through us among both the redeemed and the perishing, we are certainly functioning in this world as Aaron functioned among the Israelites. There is something about a worshipping Christian that makes people aware of life or death. Many Christians have noticed how a small group of fellow employees goes strangely silent when they join them. There is something about the fragrance of Christ in the Christian that makes the story that was being told seem badly out of place. The incense becomes a conscience to them. Incense gives them a subconscious God-awareness.

Some will silently accept this prodding of their conscience, while others will lash out in anger against it, but all can tell, without the need of our preaching to them, that they are destined for death; they are out of relationship with God. They cannot put their feelings into words, and if they did they would likely call you the "oddball," but the truth is that they are smelling something of the fragrance of God in your life, and that fragrance says, "You are not reconciled with God. Judgment is coming."

There is the other side of the coin, too. In my traveling throughout the world I constantly meet those who should be strangers to me—persons whose names I do not know and whose faces I have never seen before—and yet there is an immediate acceptance. We feel that we actually know one another, for we smell the same. We have both been in Christ's triumphal procession and have come out of it with the fragrance of life. What a delight it is to meet those whom God has set free in His abundant mercy.

Repeatedly I have witnessed troubled churches being preserved from Divine judgment by the intercessory worship of a few saints. There have been times when it seemed that there was absolutely no way the insurrecting 250 or so persons could be stopped from taking over the control of the church, but a few saints slipped into the prayer room of the church and began to worship God. The fragrance of that worship seemed to drift into the meeting hall where the politics of the church were being decided, and the presence of God stopped the rebellion on the very night it was to be consummated.

"Aaron, take incense and make an atonement!" "Church, run into the midst of the plague of sin with your worship incense to make an atonement for them!"

Perhaps there are times when our worship should leave the

sanctuary and go to the marketplace. In San Francisco, seat of homosexuality for America, there is a worshipping church whose pastor wondered what would happen if they took their worship out of the church building into the hub of homosexual activity. Each month they take their musicians, singers, dancers, and banner-carriers into the "Tenderloin" district of the city to have an open-air worship service on the street. They do not preach at or to anyone; they just begin to sing and worship the Lord right there in front of everyone. The songs are not the standard evangelistic songs normally used for open-air meetings; this group sings worship choruses and songs to the Lord.

The reaction and results have been amazing. There are repeated testimonies of homosexual couples rounding the corner locked in each other's embrace who break off physical contact when they hear and see the worship. They often come in close to watch, while tears stream down their faces. Some kneel to pray; others ask questions of church members who are positioned along the sidewalk. Some have claimed deliverance from satanic power just by watching these Christians worship. There have been numerous conversions and deliverances from homosexuality. All this is occasioned by the open worship of this congregation who dare to take the incense to the place of the plague.

Perhaps it is time for more worshipping groups to take their worship into the midst of people who are dying of the plague. The world consistently praises its master; shouldn't the Church at least occasionally worship Her Master openly? I know of a young pastor in New York State who uses the Easter and Christmas seasons to take the worship of his congregation into the marketplace. He offers the shopping malls a seasonal package with musicians, singers, and dancers, and he is rarely refused, for it is good for business. On the nights of the presentation, the entire church congregation is encouraged to be present to mingle with the spectators and to worship the Lord while the musicians and dancers are ministering to the Lord on the stage. The results have been remarkable. Worship is more than arresting; it is liberating. Most of these people would never visit a worshipping church, but when a true demonstration of worship is made available to them on their territory, they are often overwhelmed by it. They will smell the incense of God only if we, the Christians, take it out to them.

The world is dying of the plague. Are we Christians being wise in keeping our worship incense confined to the walls of our churches? That is not where the plague is; the plague is out where we work, go to school, and shop. Shouldn't the worship of our heart reach out around us everywhere we go? The people may not know what is going on, but they will become affected and protected by the incense of our worship. If we continue to keep the incense in the Holy Place, we may lose this world by default, for the plague will destroy until it comes under the influence of the incense of worship. If we let the church walls be the dividing line, then the plague of sin will wipe out the vast majority of mankind while we, the saints, are enjoying the presence of the God in the Holy Place.

What do we smell? It is possible for us to so smell the foul odor of the plague that all we talk about is that plague. Sin is rampant. Our nation is in trouble. The plague of God has broken out among us—just talk to the victims of AIDS. If something doesn't stop the plague of sin, our nation may already be skidding toward destruction. But do we have to smell the plague when God has given us censers, Divine fire, and the incense of worship? We can have a fragrance that transcends the stench of sin, and if we will share this fragrance with those smitten by sin, God may yet in mercy visit our country with His Divine presence and sweep people into the Kingdom of God. Some see only death; others see burning incense in the censers of those whom God has made to be a "kingdom of priests."

What is smelled in your home? We do not have our children around us as much as the world has them around it. What do our children smell like after a day at school? Releasing them to nearly unlimited TV viewing creates an odor of death that doesn't belong in our homes. What does dad smell on his job, and what contaminates mother during the day? Too often we gather together in the evening, defiled by what we have seen and heard all day long. The odor of the home is the stench of death that has surrounded us during the day. We need to learn the joy of burning incense before God as a family. Just taking a portion of God's Word as a topic of discussion at the table, and then rejoicing in the Lord over it, can bring the fragrance of worship into the home to replace the stench of the plague.

Parents need to cover their homes and families with the incense of worship. Workers need to cover their jobs with their offered incense, and students need to take the incense of worship into the school systems, for if we don't, the plague will destroy them, and it may also destroy us.

This is not soulwinning, nor is it an attempt to become the conscience of another. It is simply taking a worshipful spirit with us wherever we go. It is doing what Aaron did by bringing the incense to the plagued people to keep them alive until they have opportunity to return to God by the blood covenant.

There is more involved in worship than merely honoring God, for while worship brings us into the presence of God, it also brings the presence of God to others and becomes a covering for their sins and a preservation from the deserved judgment of God. We should never cease offering the incense upon the Golden Altar in the Holy Place, but we should also run with our golden censers and incense into the midst of the people dying with the plague of sin.

" 'Aaron, take a censer . . . quickly to the congregation and make atonement for them; for wrath has gone out from the LORD' " (Numbers 16:46).

Other books by K-Dimension Publishers

The Divine Runner	*Earl Paulk*
The Wounded Body of Christ	*Earl Paulk*
Ultimate Kingdom	*Earl Paulk*
Satan Unmasked	*Earl Paulk*
Sex Is God's Idea	*Earl Paulk*
Held In The Heavens Until . . .	*Earl Paulk*
To Whom Is God Betrothed?	*Earl Paulk*
The Provoker	*Tricia Weeks*
My All-Sufficient One	*Sharon Price*

For further information please contact—

P.O. Box 7300 • Atlanta, GA 30357